Apostolic Pioneering

Foreword by John Eckhardt

Apostle Stephen A. Garner

Rivers Publishing Company
Stephen A. Garner Ministries
P.O. Box 1545, Bolingbrook, IL 60440
E-mail: sagarnerministries@gmail.com
www.sagministries.com

ISBN - 978-0-9860068-1-4

Printed in the United States of America

DEDICATION

I humbly dedicate this book to Almighty God, who has truly been faithful to supply all my needs. A heartfelt thank you to my wife, Yolonda, for her steadfast support, encouragement and tireless hours of prayer; and to my mother in the Lord, Elder Bernice G. Davis, for her love and countless hours of intercession for my life and the mandate God has given me.

I want to give special thanks to Apostle John Eckhardt who is truly a modern day pioneer. The impartations received while being a part of Crusaders Church have fueled such a passion in me to advance the Kingdom of God. Thank you, Man of God, for the price you have paid with your life. May God's best continually be granted to you and your family.

FOREWORD

The church is currently seeing a global restoration of the apostle's ministry. This is being accompanied by more books being released that will help us understand and walk in this ministry correctly. The pioneering dimension of the apostle's ministry is one of the most important aspects the Church must embrace.

The church needs a revelation of the apostolic ministry and books are important to release this revelation. This book will add to the growing number of books challenging the Church to walk in present truth. Apostles are pioneers. They help to keep the Church advancing and breaking through into new territories. The Church will become stagnate without the ministry of the apostle leading in the forefront.

We need apostles to preach, teach and write their revelations. Stephen Garner has written his understanding of the pioneering dimension of the apostle's ministry. Stephen Garner is a pioneer. I have seen him pioneer new works with endurance, tenacity and boldness. His writings will encourage the next generation of apostles to emerge and fulfill their ministries.

Apostle John Eckhardt,
Crusaders Church of Chicago

INTRODUCTION

The spirit of God is breathing upon this generation and charging multitudes of believers to rise up out of the obscurity of religious, traditional, and doctrinal beliefs that have restricted God's breakthrough power from impacting their nations. This generation will be known as God's apostolic pioneers. They are presently being sent by God to chart out new pathways in the Spirit. This generation of believers is initiating Spirit-led operations to bring the Church of Jesus Christ to accurate alignment for this season of reformation.

The Kingdom of God is here and God's apostolic pioneers are positioned throughout the earth to activate its power by bringing the Church to a place of functional operation. This move of the Spirit is having lasting affects upon our societies and in those who will operate within our apostolic spheres.

I believe with all my heart that John the Baptist was an apostolic pioneer in his day. He was sent to prepare the Way for the Coming of the Lord. There were dimensions of grace active in the ministry of John the Baptist that we will see manifested in the lives of pioneers today. Jesus is set to return; yet as it was with John the Baptist, so it is with us today. A voice must prepare the Way for the Coming of the Lord.

The Life of John the Baptist was the fulfillment of prophecy. He was set apart for his assignment. He brought clarity to Jesus being the Messiah, functioned as a witness to Christ, and his ministry was a vehicle of exalting Christ and Him alone. John the Baptist was also a fearless, righteous and humble man. In the midst of a generation, full of religious control, legalism and witchcraft, John the Baptist had a grace upon his life that is definitely needed on the lives of pioneers today. John the Baptist is truly an apostolic pattern for believers today who are committed to establishing a place of entrance for the Coming of the Lord.

Apostle Stephen A. Garner

TABLE OF CONTENTS

CHAPTER 1

APOSTLES AS PIONEERS

"For as the body is one, and hath many members, and all members of that one body, being many, are one body: so also is Christ" (I Corinthians 12:12).

"Now ye are one body of Christ, and members in particular" (I Corinthians 12:27).

There is a restoration movement taking place in the church today. No true restoration can take place without pioneers coming forth. Apostles are pioneers and the Lord has set them in His Church. A pioneer is described as *"one who breaks new ground; a frontiersman, a settler of new territories, and a trendsetter."* The Bible declares the Church is the body of Christ and members in particular. Apostles are sent by God to function as ambassadors for the Church. An ambassador is a diplomat who is being sent abroad to represent his country's interests. The revelation, wisdom, strength, passion and convictions of God and His kingdom are to come through the apostle. As apostles pioneer and go into the nations of the earth, the interests and convictions of Heaven are established.

I Corinthians 12:28 declares *"that God hath set some in the church, first apostles, secondarily prophets, thirdly teachers, after that miracles, then gifts of healing, help, governments, diversities of tongues."* I want to bring attention to some important words in this verse. The first is the word *"set."* Synonyms for the word *"set"* are *"to position, plant, install, arrange, establish, place and settle."* Apostles have been positioned and established in the Church by God to implement the original and primary plan of the Lord for the Body of Christ. Apart from the operation of this gifting, the Church will become irrelevant and stagnated in kingdom dynamics.

3

The second word is *"first."* Some synonyms for the words *first* are *"in the front of, the original, initial, or primary."* Since apostles are pioneers who carry a grace to release reformation in the Church, I believe this ministry gift must begin to have a greater expression in the Church. Apostles help to advance the Church; while playing a vital role in the establishing of present truth.

God has an original plan that can only succeed when the ordained structure for the Church is modeled. Apostles and prophets are the foundations of the Church that Jesus has established. Once the Body of Christ begins to embrace this truth, we will begin to see the glory of God as we have never seen before.

I want to point out key patterns apostles must release into the local church. By no means are they conclusive; but rather an initial thrust to open our eyes to a more accurate picture of the assignment for apostolic pioneers. Apostles release grace that brings **confirmation** of the work of the local church. The grace given to apostles is especially vital in encouraging believers in the work of the ministry. The work of the ministry includes teaching, preaching, training and leadership structure. This is especially true with new church plants. There are seasons of frustration that come to hinder momentum. However, God sends apostles to keep His church consistently moving forward and current in present truth. The powers of darkness have locked up nations and the churches within these nations are lacking in present truth. This is true of many churches in America as well. Many major denominations have rejected the ministry of apostles. The churches in America struggle in various areas of doctrinal issues; such as moving in the gifts of the Spirit. As apostles lead the way to bring confirmation, the ministry of the church can expand.

4

And when they had preached the gospel to that city, and had taught many, they returned again to Lystra, and to Iconium, and Antioch, confirming the souls of the disciples, and exhorting them to continue in the faith, and that we must through much tribulation enter into the kingdom of God. And when they had ordained them elders in every church, and had prayed with fasting, they commended them to the Lord, on whom they believed (Acts 14:21-23).

There is also a God-ordained desire in the hearts of true apostles to **impart** spiritual gifts. The grace and charisma given to apostles will help establish the local church. Through apostolic impartation, divine alignment and order can be released. The gifts of the Spirit are vital in bringing forth the demonstration of the Kingdom. Many churches today are oppressed and waxing cold because of a lack of impartation. We need apostles who have a desire and knowledge on how to impart spiritual gifts. *For I long to see you, that I may impart unto you some spiritual gift, to the end ye may be established (Romans 1:11).*

Pioneers also bring **revelation** to the Church. The Apostle Paul prayed for the church of Ephesus to receive the spirit of wisdom and revelation to enlighten the eyes of their understanding. Apart from revelation released through the prayers and wisdom of apostles, the church will lack insight into kingdom mysteries. The word "revelation" means *an unveiling, uncovering or disclosure of a thing.* Proverbs 25:2 declares, *"It's the glory of God to conceal a thing: but the honor of kings to search it out."* God is not going to entrust the riches of His Kingdom to those who will not search Him out. Jesus said it is given unto us to know the mysteries of the Kingdom. Mysteries must be searched out and then the glory of God will come unto us. Revelation will give access to the armory of the Spirit needed to break through. The Church needs revelation to accurately worship and praise God, to effectively pray and intercede and to wage war against the powers of hell. Revelation will help us in applying doctrine and declaring our mandate as well.

Intercession is one of the most formidable weapons available to the Body of Christ. Apostolic intercession releases the power of God to help churches break through invisible barriers that are established by hell to restrict, hinder and frustrate believers. Apostolic pioneers carry an anointing to break limitations and dismantle the powers of darkness. Apostles must arise and begin to activate the Church in prayer; if we are going to stand in this present war. I have found that one of the ways to maintain momentum is to stay consistent in prayer. Intercession, in an apostolic church where apostles and prophets are leading the charge, is like stepping into a war zone. It is loud, violent, aggressive, authoritative and labor-inspired. The atmosphere is so spiritually charged to the point that when you leave the session, you can literally feel it in your body. We will share more on this subject in a later chapter.

Apostles are also responsible for the works in the local church, which include **maintaining order** and **proper ministry structure**. They are active in ensuring that **pure doctrine** stays pure. They are also strong advocates of **moral purity**. Apostles have a passion to advance the Kingdom by ministering throughout the nations. They function as **fathers** who release sons and daughters to plant new works in territories that are barren and undesirable. The early apostles targeted territories that were that were full of witchcraft, sorcery, debauchery and paganism. Yet, they demonstrated the superiority of the Lord Jesus over the powers of darkness. I pray for a shaking within the Church and for the Hand of the Lord to come upon us strong for the kingdom advancement.

CHAPTER 2

APOSTOLIC COMMISSION

"To open their eyes, and to turn them from darkness to light, and from the power of Satan unto God, that they may receive forgiveness of sins, and inheritance among them which are sanctified by faith that is in me" (Acts 26:18).

This passage of scripture details the commission of apostles. The word, "commission," is defined as *"a mandate, an assignment, order, charge, authority, task, duty and responsibility."* The commissioning of apostles comes from the Lord Himself. With this statement being true, our ability to articulate the assignment we have in Him is equally important. Paul is declaring his assignment to King Agrippa and quoting a prophecy from Isaiah 42:6-7.

"I the Lord have called thee in righteousness, and will hold thine hand, and will keep thee, and give thee for a covenant of the people, for a light to the Gentile; to open the blind eyes, to bring out the prisoners from the prison, and them that sat in darkness of the prison house."

This is a Messianic prophecy; yet, Paul is describing his mandate from words spoken concerning Jesus. In order for our commission to be accurate, we must consider the Chief Apostle. Hebrews 3:1 declares, *"Wherefore, holy brethren, partakers of the heavenly calling, consider the Apostle and High Priest of our profession, Christ Jesus."* Pioneers must be able to identify the works of the Lord if we are going to be successful in doing His will. This is true for all believers, especially for pioneers, in order to safeguard our missions from deception and error.

Pioneers must be able to break through as they teach and preach the word of God in order *"to open the eyes of those who are in darkness and turn them from the power of Satan unto God."* The authority and boldness on their lives will help

10

to accomplish this assignment, along with their knowledge of the scripture. Paul in Acts 13 was able to open the eyes of Sergius Palaus. Sergius was a proconsul who sought him, desiring to hear the Word of God. However, standing in his way was a certain sorcerer, a false prophet, a Jew whose name was Bar-jesus. From this passage of scripture, we can see that witchcraft, deception and religion were operating through Bar-jesus to keep Sergius Palaus blind and in darkness. Paul discerned the works of the devil in Bar-jesus and released judgment upon him. Pioneers cannot be afraid to release the judgment of God on the power of hell. This is one of several ways to open the eyes of people blind to the truth. There are multitudes of people today, in nations throughout the earth, whose eyes have been blinded to truth because of the works of darkness. The enemy does not want people to come to the knowledge of truth.

John Eckhardt states in *Apostolic Ministry*, "*Apostles are sent into regions and territories of darkness with an assignment to open the eyes of people controlled by darkness, turn them to the light and establish them in the Kingdom of God which is a kingdom of light.*" Jesus gave two different perspectives of our commission in Matthew 28 and Mark 16. Matthew 28 carries the responsibility of teaching.

"And Jesus came and spake unto them, saying, 'All power is given unto me in heaven and in earth. Go ye therefore, and teach all nations, baptizing them in the name of the Father, and of the Son and of the Holy Ghost: Teaching them to observe things whatsoever I have commanded you: and, lo, I am with you always, even unto the end of the world." Amen (Matthew 28:18-20).

The word, "teach," in this text means *to instruct with the purpose of making a disciple of the student in doctrine and*

11

conduct. One aspect of the apostolic commission is to make disciples who walk in accurate doctrine and character. Pioneers should be concerned about their disciples maintaining a lifestyle of holiness. Mark 16:15 declares, *"And He said unto them, "Go ye into all the world, and preach the gospel to every creature."* The term, "preach" is used as a catalyst for our commission. Preaching is important because it releases a grace for miracles to come forth. The gospel is the good news and it needs to be herald by forerunners, with signs following. Jesus preached and demonstrated the Kingdom of God throughout the gospels.

CHAPTER 3

SENT ONES

"Jesus saith unto them, 'My meat is to do the will of Him that sent me, and to finish his work.'" (John 4:34)

The most important aspect of apostolic ministry is centered on the term, "**Sent Ones.**" The word, "sent" is mentioned over seventy times in the New Testament alone. The understanding of this term is essential. The word, "sent" in this scripture comes from the Greek word *"apostello"* (#649) which means to *"be set apart, to send out on a mission, to send forth."* This definition applies to all believers. Every child of the Kingdom of God had a mission in life and has been sent by the Lord. Jesus prayed for us in John 17:17-18 saying, *"Sanctify them through thy truth: thy word is truth. As thou has sent me into the world even so have I also sent them into the world."* From this we can determine that Jesus is concerned about us embracing an apostolic purpose in the world unto which we are sent.

Joseph was a Sent One in his day. *"And God sent me before you to preserve you a posterity in the earth and to save your lives by a great deliverance"* (Genesis 45:7). This scripture reveals how he explained the mandate of God on his life to his family. The act of him being sold into slavery by his own brothers was actually a part of God's plan to deliver those who were living and preserve the lives of generations to come. Sent Ones must be willing to endure harshness and difficult times. The preservation and deliverance of life in our generation is a part of our mission, regardless of how difficult the journey may be. The reward of Joseph's endurance was salvation for an entire nation.

Moses had a mission to bring the children of Israel out of Egypt. He was sent by God to proclaim the Lord's name to His people and destroy the strongholds that held them captive.

"And he said, certainly I will be with thee; and this shall be a token unto thee, that I have sent thee: when thou hast brought forth the people out of Egypt, ye shall serve God upon this mountain" (Exodus 3:12).

Moses learned the ways of the Egyptians; the very ones of whom he was now sent against to bring deliverance to God's covenant people. Many believers today are ensnared by worldliness and carnality. Egypt represents the spirit of the world. We need Sent Ones to invade political, sports, entertainment, medical, educational and banking arenas; as well as other institutions of the world with signs and wonders. God is sending pioneers into the world's system to proclaim His name and deliver His people.

The walls of Jerusalem were ruined and laid in heaps of rubbish. Nehemiah represents a type of Sent One with a building grace. Building is a part of apostolic ministry. The word "build" in the Hebrew means *"to obtain children, make repairs and set up."* Nehemiah's mission was to rebuild the walls. *"And I said unto the king, if it please the king, and if thy servant hath found favor in thy sight, that thou wouldest send me unto Judah, unto the city of my fathers' sepulchers, that I may build it" (Nehemiah 2:5).* Walls represent protection, fortification and strength. Apostolic ministry provides protection and strength to cities and nations. Builders have a responsibility to make repairs and restore works of God that have suffered damage. This can be a result of rebellion towards God or an attack of the devil.

John the Baptist was a forerunner sent by God to be a witness. The word "witness" means *"to testify, certify, stand up for, and confirm."* All believers are "sent" as John the Baptist was to confirm to the world that Jesus is the Light.

"There was a man sent from God, whose name was John. The same came for a witness, to bear witness of the Light that all men through him might believe. He was not the Light, but was sent to bear witness of that Light" (John 1:6-8).

This mission is accomplished in two ways. The first is that the LIGHT is evident in our lives. The second way is for the testimony of the Lord to be in our mouth. Jesus said in John 3:19 that, "...*men love darkness rather than light because their deeds are evil.*" As we move to continue in the ways of Him that sent us and stand up for Him, the deeds of those in darkness will be rebuked and salvation can come forth.

Jesus declares, as He opens the eyes of a man born blind, his assignment is to work the works of the Sender. *"I must work the works of him that sent me while it is day: the night cometh when no man can work. As long as I am in the world I am the Light of the world" (John 9:4-5).* Our primary objective as Sent Ones must be to perform the works of He who has sent us. *"Verily, verily I say unto you, the servant is not greater than his lord; neither he that is sent greater than he that sent him" (John 13:16).* There must be a commitment within the heart of every Sent One to obey the Lord at any cost. I believe that the manifestation of the miraculous is contingent on our level of obedience. As previously stated, character and doctrine are what makes true disciples. There are multitudes of people whose eyes are blind and they have no vision of the Kingdom of God. There are those who possess tongues of the dumb that cannot speak of the things of God. Then, we have those whose ears are deaf and they do not hear the voice of God. God is sending us to them to make them whole.

Sent Ones are mandated to go and resurrect those who are dead. This implies to both physical and spiritual death. There are people who will be literally lifeless and our mission will be to raise them from the dead.

"Then they took away the stone from the place where the dead was laid. And Jesus lifted up his eyes, and said, Father, I thank thee that thou hast heard me. And I knew that thou hearest me always: but because of the people which stand by I said it, that they may believe that thou hast sent me" (John 11:41-42).

Jesus when sending the twelve charged them to raise the dead as a sign of their apostleship. Any believer who embraces the sending grace of Jesus can move in this capacity. I believe that once the full restoration of the apostle's ministry comes to fulfillment, we will experience the miraculous with greater magnitude. There are nations functioning under the powers of darkness and many of their churches are spiritually dead. Sent Ones are moving forward in the power of God and great revival and restoration are taking place. From some of the most remote locations in the world to mainstream territories, the stones of bondage are being removed and the clarion call for the dead to arise and be loosed out of death's grasp is being sounded throughout these tombs. This mass exodus and mobilization is occurring because Sent Ones are emerging!

CHAPTER 4

SIGNS
AND WONDERS

"Truly the signs of an apostle were wrought among you in all patience, in signs, wonders and mighty deeds" (II Corinthians 12:12).

There are distinctive marks that the Lord places on pioneers. Patience is the primary one. Based upon the needs and spiritual level of the people, it could take long periods of time to steer them from one place and direct them to another. The Apostle Paul abode in Corinth for a year and six months teaching the word of God in Acts 16:11. The believers of Corinth were deeply involved in idolatry and immorality, yet he labored among them in the word and many believe and worshipped God.

Signs and wonders are also evident among pioneers. *"And when he had called unto him his twelve disciples, he gave them power against unclean spirits, to cast them out, and to heal all manner to sickness and all manner of disease (Matthew 10:1).* The disciples were authorized to deal with the natural and spiritual conditions of people. Casting out devils and healing diseases are visible signs of true apostolic ministry. All believers have been commissioned to *"cast out devils and to heal the sick,"* according to Mark 16:17, yet many do not. This is why the church in every nation needs spiritual frontiersmen to emerge. Signs and wonders are also necessary in helping to bring spiritual upgrade and to break doubt and unbelief as well. Jesus said in John 4:48, *"Except you see signs and wonders, you will not believe."*

Apostolic pioneers are most damaging to the kingdom of darkness through spiritual warfare. Apostles are anointed to mobilize believers and launch mass assaults against principalities, powers, the rulers of darkness of this world and spiritual hosts of wickedness in high places. This ability, authority and responsibility are given to the apostles by the

Lord. The preaching and teaching of true apostolic pioneers disturb the powers of hell. The strongholds of darkness, the bondage of religion and the fear of man that enslave God's people are eradicated; as apostles teach, preach and prophesy.

The mighty deeds that pioneers perform are contingent on their proficiency in the Word. The religious leaders in the Lord's Day were bewildered by His knowledge of the Word. Although, He was not affiliated with any of their schools, He was superior in word and in deed. *"And they were astonished at his doctrine: for He taught them as one that had authority, and not as the scribes" (Mark 1:22).* Mighty deeds today require skill in the Word of God. Apostles possess strength in the Word and are able to perform mighty deeds for the Lord. Most believers who struggle to break through become skilled in their assignment once they connect to an apostolic work. *"And Moses was learned in all the wisdom of the Egyptians, and was mighty in words and in deeds" (Acts 7:22).* The mandate of pioneers warrants that they are strong in the Word of God. The Lord upholds all things by the word of His power, according to Hebrews 1:3. The key principle that distinguishes pioneers from those who are experts of the letter of the Word is the spiritual authority that they carry. The letter kills but the Spirit gives life. Therefore, by the Spirit of God, mighty deeds are executed through the hands of pioneers.

Moses was a man used of God to establish His law. Signs and wonders were a part of his ministry as it was with Jesus. Moses had an assignment to introduce God to His people and the task of delivering them from the bondage of slavery in Egypt. This task could not be accomplished without a manifestation of mighty deeds. A rod was given to Moses as a sign of authority to execute the plan of God. Moses' rod also symbolized the rule of Christ. Pioneers must know how to release the rule of Christ. He used it to bring judgment on the powers of darkness. Through Moses, God destroyed the economic system of Egypt. Their water was turned into blood. Frogs, lice and swarms of flies invaded the lands and citizens of Egypt. An army of locusts and a hailstorm devastated their crops. The livestock of Egypt was destroyed. Darkness filled the land and boils came upon the Egyptians. God then sends an angel to destroy the firstborn of Egypt. These plagues of judgment were all mighty deeds of God through a pioneering people, breaking the oppressive powers that are holding the saints captive.

CHAPTER 5

APOSTOLIC INTERCESSION

"Pray without ceasing" (I Thessalonians 5:17).

What began with prayer in the Upper Room must continue in our generation and the generations to come. There were 120 believers gathered praying for ten consecutive days for the Promise of the Holy Spirit. As they continued, suddenly there came a sound from heaven as a rushing mighty wind and the appearance of cloven tongues of fire, and it sat upon each of them. This corporate prayer meeting of apostles and believers activated a release from Heaven, which changed the destiny of the earth from that day forward.

There is a common thread of intercession being released by the apostles and other believers throughout the Acts of the Apostles. As they pioneered in their mission to progress the plan of salvation for the earth, great grace was extended to them because of their intercession. Apostolic intercession is vital in times of transition and reform. The word "intercession" means *"to intercede for, to change upon by conferring with, and to entreat in favor against."* We are charged by the Lord to favor His righteous cause and to also resist the devil. I believe that by our declarations, made through intercession, we can activate this principle. There is also a strength released to resist the devil as we remain steadfast in intercession.

The Apostle Peter represents the move of God essential for a release of new grace. Persecution was increasing in the land and political treachery was mounting. There was also a famine in the land and much distress among the people. Much attention was suddenly directed toward the church and Herod began to kill the apostles. James, the brother of John, lost his life as a martyr. Peter was also about to be destroyed by Herod, but the church began to pray. They prayed without ceasing. They stretched out and extended themselves in prayer. *"Peter therefore was kept in prison: but prayer was made without ceasing of the church unto God for him" (Acts 12:5).* As the saints prevailed with their intercession, the Angel of the Lord was released from heaven and delivered the apostle from prison. Pioneers can rest assured in the fact that as we advance God's purpose, angelic protection through intercession is available. Peter was freed from jail and delivered from death.

During times of the distress and unrest in our cities and nations, people should be able to turn to the church and receive of the Lord. It takes a pioneering spirit to press forward when adversity and hostilities manifest. I am persuaded that if we do not begin to stretch out and extend ourselves in intercession during times of shifting and transition, we could suffer the loss of key leaders as did the early church. The intercession of the saints at that time was truly groundbreaking. They overturned the decree of Herod the King and released the grace of God to bring forth a new move of God. We discover in Acts 12 that divine judgment was released upon Herod. The Angel of the Lord destroyed him and the Word of God grew and multiplied. Through corporate intercession, the Church advanced and caused a shifting in the natural. What was to be a dark and destructive time for the Church gave birth to a glorious victory!

"And at midnight Paul and Silas prayed, and sang praises unto God: and the prisoners heard them. And suddenly there was a great earthquake, so that the foundations of the prison were shaken: and immediately all the doors were opened, and every ones bands were loosed" (Acts 16:25-26)

"Let the high praises of God be in their mouth, and a two-edged sword in their band; To execute vengeance upon the heathen, and punishment upon the people; To bind their kings with

chains, and their nobles with fetters of iron; To execute upon them the judgment written: this honour have all his saints. Praise ye the LORD" (Psalms 149:6-9).

There are two points we must acknowledge, in order to capitalize on what occurred in Acts 16:25-26. They are, the hour in which they gathered and the pattern of prayer and singing praises unto God. Midnight is the transitioning watch that shows the exit of one day and the beginning of the next. As we embrace praying and praising God at strategic times corporately, God can bring the power needed for dismantling demonic strongholds that keep up captive; and initiate the release of liberty ordained for us in Christ.

The prayers of pioneers are destructive against satanic foundations that support strongholds of bondage. A critical key in identifying true apostolic pioneers is discerning the strength of their prayer life. Their intercession should carry enough power to literally break the supporting systems of wickedness that holds people captive. There are many who are locked up with various types of bondage and often, it is difficult for them to hear the message of the gospel. However, I believe that as intercession, coupled with the release of celebratory praise going forth, freedom will come to many.

As we begin to see apostolic and prophetic leaders do this, more of the kingdom of darkness will be shaken in our cities. There are some things that God desires to release to His church and our response to Him in prayer is vital. *"For I know that this shall turn to my salvation through your prayer, and the supply of the Spirit of Jesus Christ" (Philippians 1:19).* God's desire is that salvation comes into the earth. It will be through our intercession that the supply lines of heaven are connected to our cities, territories and nations. This, in turn, will bring forth the supply of the Spirit of Jesus Christ. May

the grace of God to fervently pray and praise Him abound in
the lives of pioneers, as we advance the Kingdom of God.

CHAPTER 6

ESTABLISH NEW INITIATIVES

Apostolic believers are given a grace and an anointing to initiate new endeavors. The word, "initiate" means *"to begin and set in motion, to instruct a person in a subject."* Apostolic initiators are necessary in order to establish new spiritual territories and maintain momentum during difficult times. There is a joy that comes to initiators when those within our sphere began to get established, instructed and activated in the kingdom of God.

Abram is a type of initiator. He is given a charge by God to depart from his father's house, a place of familiarity. Now the Lord has said unto Abram,

"Get thee out of thy country and from thy kindred and from thy father's house and unto a land that I will show thee. So Abram departed, as the Lord had spoken unto him; and Lot went with him: and Abram was seventy and five years old when he departed out of Haran" (Genesis 12:1,4).

His home, Haran, was an idolatrous capital and his family was indifferent to the call on his life. He was not given a direct destination for his journey. He was just charged to go to a place that he would be shown. The establishing of new things and places in God require absolute obedience. Abram's obedience actually set into motion the plan of God that is still impacting the generations of the righteous today.

Abram did not have an idea what things he and his family were going to face. He was an ordinary man with common issues like many of us today. Yet, he was chosen by God to begin a new apostolic work. The course of his life has become a pattern to many who are divinely inspired by God to pioneer new works. Many believers are being stirred to move to a new place in the Spirit. As our faith level rises to help undergird the obedience we are called to embrace, greater levels of expansion, upgrade and an increase of influence will come upon our lives.

"And there was a famine in the land, beside the first famine that was in the days of Abraham. And Isaac went unto Abimelech king of the Philistines unto Gerar. And the LORD appeared unto him, and said, Go not down into Egypt; dwell in the land which I shall tell thee of: Sojourn in this land, and I will be with thee, and will bless thee; for unto thy seed, I will give all these countries, and I will perform the oath which I sware unto Abraham thy father; And I will make thy seed to multiply as the stars of heaven, and will give unto thy seed all these countries; and in thy seed shall all the nations of the earth be blessed; Because that Abraham obeyed my voice, and kept my charge, my commandments, my statutes, and my laws. And Isaac dwelt in Gerar" (Genesis 26:1-6)

God instructs Isaac to dwell among the Philistines in the city of Gerar. Because of the covenant promise made to his father, Abraham, Isaac was able to dwell and prosper in Gerar. Covenant relationships are vital in carrying out the mandate of the Lord. The grace necessary to remain and withstand in a new place is based upon our willingness to live through a covenant relationship with God. When we are faithful to walk out the patterns for us as pioneers, the Lord will surely partner with us and our seed. Through our divine partnership with God, His goodness is released in our lives. Abraham's obedience and Isaac's diligence, coupled with God's purpose to give him the land, proved to be destructive against the powers of darkness in Gerar.

The grace to prevail that rested upon Isaac eventually led King Abimelech to acknowledge the tremendous presence of God in Isaac's life. Genesis 26:16 declares, *"And Abimelech said unto Isaac, Go from us: for thou art much mightier than we.*" The days of enemy combatants testifying of our strength to overtake territories are upon us; as we continue where we are assigned and abide in the place where He sends us. Absolute obedience is essential in overthrowing established orders and initiating the Kingdom of God in the earth. Let us learn the value of covenant in spite of initial indifferences, we will encounter in the works we do. The Almighty God who dwells in us is much mightier than they that are against us.

CHAPTER 7

POSSESS A WARRING SPIRIT

"The Lord is a man of war: the Lord is his name" Exodus 15:3

"The Lord shall go forth as a mighty man; he shall stir up jealousy like a man of war: he shall cry, yea roar, he shall prevail against his enemies" Isaiah 42:13.

Names are very important in the scriptures. They carry a twofold purpose in revealing the nature of a person and their destiny. For instance, the name "Joseph," means *"Jehovah Has Given Increase."* Joseph was sent by God to preserve a nation and through the completion of this assignment, he also brought increase into Egypt during a time of famine. His name carried a strong prophetic significance. I believe that as often as he was called Joseph, it fortified his assignment of being a conduit for the increase of Jehovah.

The scriptural foundation of this chapter gives us insight into the nature of God. He is a Man of War. If we are to advance His Kingdom into regions governed by strongholds of darkness, we must possess a warring spirit and be assured that our God is a man of war as well. Robert Gay writes in his book, *Silence the Enemy*, "The level of maturity and fellowship you attain in God will be in direct proportion of your revelation of Him. A person who does not have a revelation of Jehovah Rapha, *'The God Who Heals,'* will not get healed." Likewise, without the revelation of Jess as "The Warrior-The Lord of Host," we will not be able to wage successful spiritual warfare.

David is a type of an apostolic pioneer who possessed a warring spirit. David was a man acquainted with the nature of God; he was a worshipper, a man after God's own heart. I believe intimacy is paramount in order to understanding the ways of God, but knowing when to move in them is just as equally important. For those who have developed a skill in warfare; I believe will agree that having the heart of a warrior is their greatest asset, along with their intimate connection with God. As a pioneer, I have found that keeping my heart pliable and maintaining a balance of worship and praise has afforded me many victories where my knowledge of warfare could have never done alone.

David was known for the many battles he won in the Lord. There were songs sang and his notoriety spread abroad. I believe he is best known for destroying the Philistine champion, Goliath. This victory set precedence for him. As David had to contend with giants in his day, we must do so in our day. Today, nations are bound with occultism, powers of witchcraft, false religion, pride, deception and confusion. These are some of the giants of our day that have positioned themselves in the heavenly realms over our cities. My prayer is for God to release warring pioneers in our land to confront and utterly destroy them.

In Joel 2:4-11, the Prophet Joel describes a swarm of locusts as agents of God's judgment. These locusts were sent by God to execute His Will upon a rebellious people. Prophetically, I believe that God will raise up a pioneering people who are skilled in warfare that will execute His judgment upon the powers of hell within the nations of the earth.

"The appearance of them is as the appearance of horses; and as horsemen, so shall they run. Like the noise of chariots on the tops of mountains shall they leap, like the noise of a flame of fire that devoureth the stubble, as a strong people set in battle array" (Joel 2:4-6).

These pioneers who are coming forth in this generation will possess the same abilities in warfare, as this army described

33

by Joel. He is proclaiming that this army will initiate the Day of the Lord and create new pathways to establish new beginnings in the nations for the Lord Jesus Christ. Let us look at the grace that God releases upon them. I believe that this army will have tremendous stamina and strength. The word, "stamina" means *"physical or mental endurance."* Believers who have warring spirits must have an anointing to endure. Paul told Timothy,

"Therefore endure hardness, as a good soldier of Jesus Christ. No man that warreth himself with the affairs of their life; that he may please him who hath chosen him to be a soldier" (II Timothy 2:3-4).

Soldiers in the Army of God, who will execute judgment on the prince of this world, must not be yoked to this world. Their affections must be for the Kingdom of God. Those who will be used to advance the Kingdom must live by strong convictions to further the purposes of God. Joel declares in verse 7 that "they shall not break rank." *"They shall run like mighty men; they shall climb the wall like men of war; and they shall march every one on his ways, and they shall not beak their ranks."* This means that these believers are committed to the pursuit of corporate unity. They are moving together with a common mission to fulfill God's agenda.

"Neither shall one thrust another, they shall walk everyone in his path." In Verse 8, the word, "thrust", has a peculiar meaning. It means *"to depress, oppress, or vex."* Oftentimes, when the Spirit of God releases new movements, men arise and fight, oppress and vex those pioneers who are initiating His new works. Nevertheless, this army of believers will move to complete the assignments and tasks that they were sent to do. The latter portion of this scripture describes the durability of this new breed of warriors. *"And when they fall*

34

upon the sword, they shall not be wounded" (Joel 2:8). This scripture reiterates that when they fall upon the sword, they shall not be wounded. I believe that this end-time army that God is mobilizing today will have tremendous resilience. It is said that those who live by the sword shall die by the sword. This statement holds true to those who live in spiritual error. But God promises this army of believers will not be wounded "when they fall upon the sword". There is an anointing being released to establish resilience in the Church. Those who know how to "bounce back" will quickly regain their posture in the heat of the battle. As the battleground is being staged for the end-time war for souls, we will see opponents and attacks that we have never faced before. Yet, God is releasing new weaponry and skills to equip His prophetic army in worship, praise and intercession. These will be catapults to bring about the manifestations of the Day of the Lord.

CHAPTER 8

ATTRIBUTES OF PIONEERS

In closing, I would like to describe several attributes ascribed to those who are pioneers. In order to prevent abuse and deception, we must clearly define the character and conduct befitting pioneers.

Pioneers are anointed to stir, motivate, activate, challenge, release, provoke, equip and train leaders to fulfill Kingdom mandates.

"And the LORD stirred up the spirit of Zerubbabel the son of the Shealtiel, governor of Judah, and the spirit of Joshua the son of Josedech, the high priest, and the spirit of all the remnant of the people; and they came and did work in the house of the LORD of hosts, their God," (Haggai 1:14).

"Wherefore I put thee in remembrance that thou stir up the gift of God, which is in thee by the putting on of my hands" (II Timothy 1:6).

Pioneers build works that leave a spiritual inheritance and legacy for future generations.

"A good man leaveth an inheritance to his children's children: and the wealth of the sinner is laid up for the just" (Proverbs 13:22).

Pioneers establish and set accurate Government.

"And in those days, when the number of the disciples was multiplied, there arose a murmuring of the Grecians against the Hebrews, because their widows were neglected in the daily ministration. Then the twelve called the multitude of the disciples unto them, and said it is not reason that we should leave the word of God, and serve tables. Wherefore, brethren, look yet out among you seven men of honest report, full of the

Holy Ghost and wisdom, whom we may appoint over this business. But we will give ourselves continually to prayer, and to the ministry of the word" (Acts 6:1-4)

Pioneers are visionary people who are graced to see beyond temporal realms and access eternal patterns.

"Where there is no revelation, the people cast off restraint; but blessed is he who keeps the law" (Proverbs 29:18).

"I will stand upon my watch, and set me upon the tower, and will watch to see what he will say unto me, and what I shall answer when I am reproved. And the LORD answered me, and said, Write the vision, and make it plain upon tables, that he may run that readeth it. For the vision is yet for an appointed time, but at the end it shall speak, and not lie: though it tarry, wait for it; because it will surely come, it will not tarry" (Habakkuk 2:1-3).

Pioneers, lead by God's glory, reveal the way for those to whom they are sent.

"And they took their journey from Succoth, and encamped in Etham, in the edge of the wilderness. And the Lord went before them by day in a pillar of a cloud, to lead them the way; and by night in a pillar of fire, to give them light; to go by day and night: He took not away the pillar of the cloud by day, nor the pillar of fire by night, from before the people" (Exodus 13:20-22).

Pioneers are concerned about God's work appearing in the lives of the saints.

Let thy work appear unto thy servants, and thy glory unto their children. And let the beauty of the LORD our God be upon us:

and establish thou the work of our hands upon us; yea, the work of our hands establish thou it" (Psalms 90:16-17).

Pioneers enlighten those who are limited in revelation of the doctrine of the Lord.

"And they were astonished at his doctrine: for he taught them as one that had authority, and not as the scribes" (Mark 1:22).

Pioneers know how to identify the strongholds of darkness and demolish them.

"For though we walk in the flesh, we do not war after the flesh: For the weapons of our warfare are not carnal, but mighty through God to the pulling down of strongholds; Casting down imaginations, and every high thing that exalteth itself against the knowledge of God, and bringing into captivity every thought to the obedience of Christ" (II Corinthians 10:3-5).

Pioneers are graced to perform under pressure.

"But when the Philistines heard that they had anointed David, King over Israel, all the Philistines came up to seek David; and David heard of it, and went down to the hold. The Philistines also came and spread themselves in the valley of Rephaim. And David enquired of the LORD, saying, Shall I go up to the Philistines? Wilt thou deliver them into mine hand? And the LORD said unto David, Go up: for I will doubtless deliver the Philistines into thine hand. And David came to Baalperazim, and David smote them there, and said, The LORD hath broken forth upon mine enemies before me, as the breach of waters. Therefore he called the name of the place Baalperazim" (II Samuel 5:17-20).

Pioneers will not defile themselves for the world's substance, status, or rewards.

"But Daniel purposed in his heart that he would not defile himself with the portion of the king's meat, not with the wine which he drank: therefore he requested of the prince of the eunuchs that he might not defile himself" (Daniel 1:8).

Pioneers are not afraid to suffer to bring forth the things of God.

"For I reckon that the sufferings of this present time are not worthy to be compared with the glory which shall be revealed in us" (Romans 8:18).

Pioneers carry impartation that release spiritual gifting.

"For I long to see you, that I may impart unto you some spiritual gift, to the end ye may be established," (Romans 1:11).

By no means, is this an exhaustive list of attributes. However, these twelve are vital for pioneers to be fruitful and accomplish their assignment. Therefore, I want to encourage you to pray fervently and ask the Lord to reveal His plan for your life as an apostolic pioneer so that Kingdom advancement can function in you in a greater capacity.

More Great Resources from
Stephen A. Garner Ministries

Books
- Benefits of Praying in Tongues
- Exposing the Spirit of Anger
- Fundamentals of Deliverance 101, Revised and Expanded
- Ministering Spirits: "Engaging the Angelic Realm"
- Pray Without Ceasing, Special Edition
- Restoring Prophetic Watchmen
- Essentials of the Prophetic Revised & Expanded
- Deliver Us From Evil
- The Kingdom of God: A Believer's Guide to Kingdom Living
- Kingdom Prayer
- Prayers, Decrees and Confessions for Wisdom
- Prayers, Decrees and Confessions for Favour & Grace
- Prayers, Decrees and Confessions for Prosperity
- Prayers, Decrees and Confessions for Increase
- Prayers, Decrees and Confessions for Righteousness, Revised & Expanded
- Prayers, Decrees and Confessions for Goodness & Mercy
- Prayers, Decrees and Confessions for Power
- Prayers that Strengthen Marriages and Families

CD's
- Prayers For The Nations
- Prayers Against Python & Witchcraft
- Prayers Of Healing & Restoration
- Prayers of Renunciation and Deliverance
- Thy Kingdom Come
- The Glory
- Latter Rain
- Overcoming Spirits of Terrorism
- Songs of Intercession
- The Spirit of the Breaker
- The Fear of The Lord

Contact Information
Stephen A. Garner Ministries
P.O. Box 1545, Bolingbrook, IL 60440
Email: sagarnerministries@gmail.com
www.sagministries.com

www.ingramcontent.com/pod-product-compliance
Lightning Source LLC
LaVergne TN
LVHW051204080426
835508LV00021B/2804